GRUMPY CAT
GOES TO SCHOOL
Mini Coloring Book

John Kurtz

DOVER PUBLICATIONS, INC.
Mineola, New York

Grumpy Cat's day begins with an alarm clock and ends with homework—a typical school day. But Grumpy's day is anything but typical! Who else would give a bus driver a cactus as a gift, frown on Picture Day, hate finger painting, or end up in a recycling bin? Grumpy Cat, that's who! Find out what other adventures Grumpy Cat has at school, and have a grumpy time coloring the pictures in this fun little book.

Grumpy Cat and Related Artwork © and ® Grumpy Cat Limited
www.GrumpyCats.com Used Under License

Illustrations by John Kurtz

Bibliographical Note

Grumpy Cat Goes to School Mini Coloring Book is a new work, first published by Dover Publications, Inc., in 2017.

International Standard Book Number

ISBN-13: 978-0-486-81960-0
ISBN-10: 0-486-81960-4

Manufactured in the United States by LSC Communications
81960402   2020
www.doverpublications.com

Wake Up!

1

Shower

Breakfast

Gift for the Bus Driver

Fun On the Bus

SCHOOL BUS

Crossing Guard

School Locker

Class Supplies

Apple for the Teacher

Anatomy

Computer Class

Sunny Day

Swing Fun

Juice Box Snack

Fire House Field Trip

Presentation

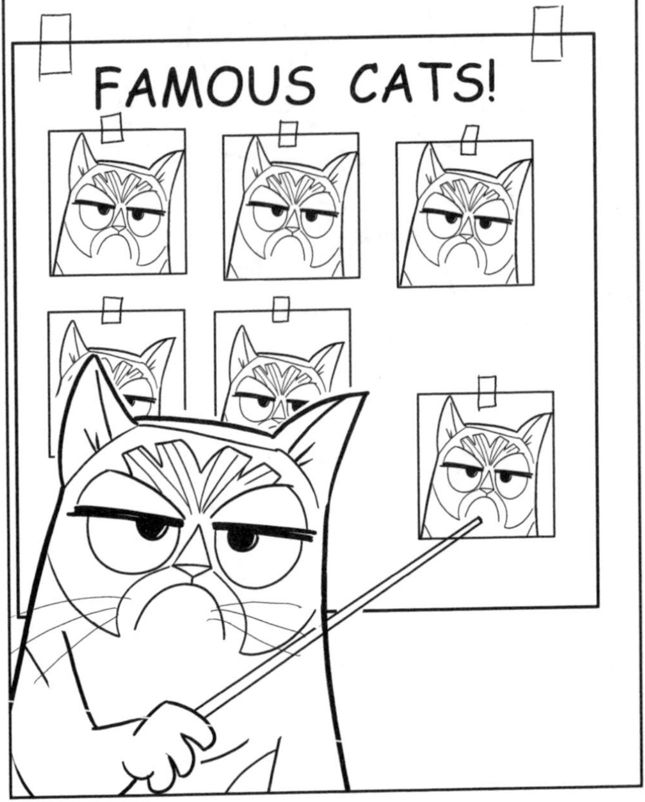

Class Choir

Baseball

Geography Class

Class Fish Tank

Easter Parade

Blocks

Rainy Day

Staying Inside

Music Class

Class Plant

Math Class

31

Valentine

Pottery Class

Finger Painting

Class Garden

Dance Class

Goalie

Lunch

History Class

Gym Class

Jumping Rope

Visit to the Museum

43

Lab
Class

44

Volcano Experiment

Detention

Recycling

Lesson in ELECTRICITY

Award Day

Slide Fun

Teeter Totter

Spelling Bee

Art Class

Grumpy Birthday

Moving Up Day

3 Points

Cheer for the Team

School Play

Scouting

Waiting for the Bus

Making Friends on the Bus

Homework